Kids Say the Funniest Things

Always an LOL* Moment

*Laugh out loud

Publications International, Ltd.

Contributing Writers:
Holli Fort hails from an incredibly large yet amazingly functional and funny family. Despite this, or maybe because of it, she developed a peculiar sense of humor that she is busy instilling in her three young sons.

Angela Hampt-Sanchez is a proud mother of seven and delighted grandmother of nine. She has traveled extensively through 42 of the 50 United States by car and has found humor all along the way—in parenting, grandparenting, and traveling.

Comedy writer **Paul Seaburn** believes that laughter keeps him young, no matter what his driver's license photo implies. Paul writes comedy for television, radio, the Web, humor books, magazines, and comedians. He's the head writer for a jazz-blues-and-comedy show on public radio. You can find more info and more laughs at www.humorhandyman.com.

Illustrations: Dennis Cox/Shutterstock.com

ISBN-13: 978-1-4508-3150-5
ISBN-10: 1-4508-3150-8

Manufactured in China.

8 7 6 5 4 3 2 1

Maybe with the Right Middle Name

I hadn't realized that my five-year-old son had overheard his mother and me discussing the new baby until my dad stopped by for a visit.

"Are you excited about a baby brother or sister coming?" he asked my son.

"I guess so, Grandpa. But I think the names Daddy has picked out are kind of weird. He said if it's a girl he would like to name her Elizabeth, and that's okay, I suppose. But if it's another boy, Daddy said they are definitely going to call it Quits."

My friend's daughter came home from school very upset, and said, "Emma says you're the tooth fairy! Is that true?" My friend was caught off guard and said, "Well, yes," and her daughter cried, "Mo-om! How could you go out every night like that and leave us here alone?"

—SAIREY GAMP

The Sunday school teacher asked the class, "What did Mary say when she found Jesus in the temple?"

Pat raised his hand.

"She said, 'I thought you were Catholic.'"

A Real Mix-Up

Hoping to buy a minute's peace at the checkout line of the grocery store, Mike bought each of his kids a bag of M&M's candies. The kids ripped into the bags, and there were about ten seconds of blessed silence before a shrill cry of distress came: "Daddy!"

"What's wrong, honey?"

"There's something wrong with my candy! I need a new bag!" cried his daughter.

"What's wrong with them?"

"They're all Ws!"

Dear God,

Thank you for my baby brother, but what I prayed for was a puppy.

Signed, Joyce

"I am such a loser!" my son Evan exclaimed.

"No you're not!" I said firmly. "Why would you think such a thing?"

"I lost my ball, I lost my action figure, and I lost my favorite truck... I lose *everything*!"

Two little boys walk into a bar. The bartender says, "We don't serve minors here."

The one boy turned to the other and said, "I told you we should have left our shovels in the sandbox."

❀   ❀   ❀

Little Brother: "If you broke your arm in two places, what would you do ?"

Big Brother: "I wouldn't go back to those two places, that's for sure."

❀   ❀   ❀

SONGS THE BEATLES WROTE WHEN THEY WERE KIDS:

· · · · · · · · · · · · · · · · · · · ·

- I Wanna Hold Your Candy
- Hey Dude
- Lucy in the Yard with Dandelions
- Here Comes the Mom
- Strawberry Jelly Forever
- All You Need Is Gum
- Salt and Pepper's Only for My Dad
- Eight Naps a Week
- You've Got to Put Your Toys Away
- Back in the Rear of Mom's Car

Danny was bored one day and started looking through the books on his mom's bookshelf. He found a leaf pressed between two pages and immediately ran off to find his mother.

"Mom, Mom! Can we go to church?" When his mom asked why, Danny replied: "That guy Adam? In the painting? I just found his underwear!"

A Sunday School teacher asked, "Johnny, do you think Noah did a lot of fishing when he was on the Ark?"

"No," replied Johnny. "How could he, with just two worms?"

I Concur

On the first day of school, the teacher wrote this sentence on the whiteboard to test how much her students had retained over the summer: "I ain't had no fun since school started." She then asked, "How would I correct this?"

Billy put his hand up and was the first one called on to answer. "Well, if it was me, Mrs. Simon, I would just quit coming here, but my mom won't let me."

"How many parents does it take to change a lightbulb?" Maggie asked Will. "Two," he replied. "One to change the bulb and one to yell 'Stop swearing or you'll wake the kids!'"

❀   ❀   ❀

Father: "I hear you skipped school to play football."

Son: "No, I didn't. I have the fish to prove it!"

❀   ❀   ❀

When your mother is mad and asks you, "Do I look stupid?" it's best not to answer her.

—MEGHANN, AGE 13

❀   ❀   ❀

I was struggling to get the last bit of ketchup out of the bottle one day when the phone rang, so I asked my four-year-old daughter to answer it and ask whomever it was if I might call them back later. This was her end of the conversation: "Mommy can't talk to you right now, Father Clark. She's busy hitting the bottle."

At Sunday school, the lesson of the day was the story of Lot's wife. The teacher explained to the kids, "God told Lot to flee the city with his wife and never look back, but his wife didn't listen, and she was turned into a pillar of salt."

The kids were silent for a minute, then Gracie raised her hand. "But what happened to the flea?"

Each generation has been
an education for us in different ways.
The first child-with-bloody-nose was
rushed to the emergency room.
The fifth child-with-bloody-nose was
told to go to the yard immediately and
stop bleeding on the carpet.

—ART LINKLETTER

Billy's Guide to Things You Shouldn't Do with Milk:

- Try to pour it back into the carton

- Drink it through a paper towel tube

- Fill the bathtub with it so you can dunk giant cookies

- Use it to cover what you spilled on a white rug

- Drink it while watching a funny television show

A Most Sincere Apology

What is it about boys who won't stop fighting? Mine are five and six and are at each other's throats constantly.

One day, I overheard an argument that ended with the younger one calling the older one a dummy. I immediately put him in time-out, where he cried his eyes out at the indignity. Afterward, I made him apologize to his brother.

Reluctantly, he finally choked out, "I'm sorry you're such a dummy!"

The restaurant where our family went for lunch one Sunday was crowded because of a big NFL game on television. The busy server took our order, but quite a while went by before she even brought our drinks. Just as she was setting them down, loud cheering broke out from across the room. "Hey," commented my 12-year-old, "I guess someone finally got their food."

Love is the most important thing in the world, but baseball is pretty good too.

—GREG, AGE 8

I take my children everywhere, but they always find their way back home.

—ROBERT ORBEN

My son was notorious for being the class clown. When the substitute teacher asked his name, he answered "Spider-Man"—to his classmates' delight. The substitute didn't find it quite as funny and demanded to know his real name. My son apologized: "Oh, I'm sorry. It's Peter Parker."

After a long day, I finally got a chance to sit down with a glass of wine. "Whew, I'm pooped!" I told my husband.

"Oh no, Mommy!" exclaimed my daughter. "In your pants?"

If you are surrounded by sea you are an island. If you don't have sea all round you, you are incontinent.

—WAYNE, AGE 7

BOOKS BY FAMOUS AUTHORS WHEN THEY WERE KIDS

- Ernest Hemingway: *I Like to Smell Trolls*
- John Steinbeck: *The Grapes Are Sour*
- Kurt Vonnegut: *I Count to Five*
- Leo Tolstoy: *Warmed-Up Peas*
- Fyodor Dostoevsky: *Crying and Punishment*
- Stephen Crane: *The Red Bag of Chocolate*
- Jonathan Swift: *Gulliver Crosses the Street*
- Alex Comfort: *The Joy of Socks*

Give Me a Sign!

Sign on back of minivan: "Babies on board. Beep all you want—I can't hear a thing."

Sign on back of baby stroller: "Potty train ing in progress: This stroller makes frequent stops."

Well, When You Put It That Way

I received a call from my son's teacher. It seems that not only did he turn in the same report entitled "My Dog" that his brother had written for the same teacher a year earlier, but he also gave a rather sarcastic reply when asked why he would attempt to do such a foolish thing.

"Oh, I am sorry, Mrs. Tyler. What exactly did he say to you?" I asked.

His teacher told me he had the nerve to say, "Well, of course it's the same report, it's the same dog, isn't it?"

✿   ✿   ✿

"Daaaad, Billy took a name insane!"

"What are you talking about, Sam?"

"Billy took a name insane! He said 'God' but you're supposed to say 'gosh!'"

What you remember about vacation: We took the kids to see the Grand Canyon, and on the way back we stopped and played with the world's largest ball of yarn. It was an experience they'll never forget!

What your six-year-old writes for his school assignment: I remember when we went to Arizona. We went to a restaurant and ate pizza!

"What's the most dangerous flower in the garden?" Chuckie asked Wendy.

"I give up," Wendy replied. Chuckie pointed and said, "That one over there with the pistil."

If your sister hits you,
don't hit her back. Parents always
catch the second person.

—MICHAEL, AGE 10

Bobby and Sally were playing doctor and nurse with a headless Barbie doll. "This doll needs a new head," diagnosed Dr. Bobby.

"She wants a second opinion," said Nurse Sally.

"OK," said Dr. Bobby, "She needs to let Ken drive her Corvette once in a while."

23

Helen took her son, Jackson, to meet her old college roommate for lunch.

"You are so cute I could just eat you up!" said Jane to Jackson.

"I am NOT on the menu!" Jackson scowled indignantly.

Love is when you go out to eat and give somebody most of your French fries without making them give you any of theirs.

—CHRISSY, AGE 6

BILLY'S GUIDE TO LEAST POPULAR SUMMER CAMPS

• •

- Camp Fun with Fractions
- Camp Friends of Veggies
- Camp Clean-a-Lot
- Camp Dances but No Wolves
- Camp Looks Good on Your College Application

My young grandson called the other day to wish me Happy Birthday. He asked me how old I was, and I told him, "62." He was quiet for a moment, and then he asked, "Did you start at 1?"

My son came to me one day and asked if he would ever have a little sister. I was so happy, since his father and I had wondered when to share our big news with him. "Oh, dear, do you really want a little sister?"

"I sure do, Mommy," Sean replied earnestly. "I'm tired of teasing the cat—sometimes he scratches me."

There are only two things a child will share willingly—communicable diseases and its mother's age.

—BENJAMIN SPOCK

SONGS THE ROLLING STONES WROTE WHEN THEY WERE KIDS:

• • • • • • • • • •

- Jumping Rope Fast
- You Can Always Get What You Want (If You Cry)
- Painted Blocks
- Get Off of My Couch
- Let's Spend My Dime Together
- Little Red Diaper
- Feet Stinkin' Man

I stopped believing in Santa Claus when I was six. Mother took me to see him in a department store and he asked for my autograph.

—SHIRLEY TEMPLE

"Mom, can we get a new video game?" asked Wyatt.

"We'll see," came my absentminded reply from the front of the minivan.

"What does that even mean?" Wyatt asked in frustration.

"It means she doesn't want to tell you no until we're home so she can send you to your room if you throw a fit!" replied his older sister from the backseat.

If mom says "no," she means it.
If dad says "no," it means maybe.

—JOSEPH, AGE 13

Beauty is skin deep. But how rich you are can last a long time.

—CHRISTINE, AGE 9

On a long overdue visit to his hometown, Bruce tried to get to know his nephew better.

"So, Johnny, what do you think you'll be once you graduate?"

Johnny thought for a while, then replied, "An old man."

Alien Bait

Four-year-old Alex was really excited to go on his first fishing trip with his grandpa. Grandpa had explained to him the whole process, starting with looking under rocks and digging up some good bait. Alex searched the ground long and hard, and finally came up with a beetle. He proudly showed it to his grandpa.

"Sorry, Alex, that one won't do—it's not an earthworm."

"Really, Grandpa? What planet is it from?"

I'm not rushing into being in love. I'm finding fourth grade hard enough.

—REGINA, AGE 10

"**G**od is invisible," announced my four-year-old daughter.

"No, he's not!" sneered her five-year-old brother.

"Yes, he is!" my daughter insisted. "It says it right in the Pledge of Allegiance: 'Under God, who is invisible, with liberty and justice for all.'"

"Okay, Penny," said Mom, "we're going to get our nails done and then go out to lunch."

"But why, Mom? You said we could get lunch first!"

"I've changed my mind."

"Oh," said Penny. "Does it work better now?"